Daddy wears Speedos

sexy

/ˈsɛksi/

adjective

1. 1.

sexually attractive or exciting.

"sexy French underwear"

synonyms:

sexually attractive, seductive, desirable, alluring, inviting, sensual, sultry, slinky, provocative, tempting, tantalizing; More

•

1. 2.

INFORMAL

very exciting or appealing.

"business magazines might not seem like the sexiest career choice"

synonyms:

exciting, stimulating, interesting, appealing, intriguing;

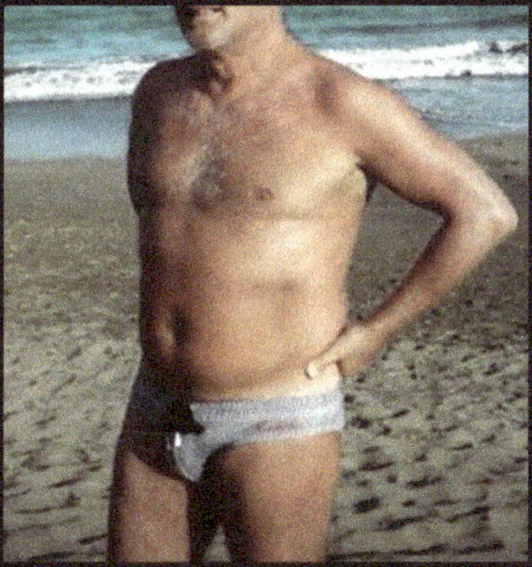

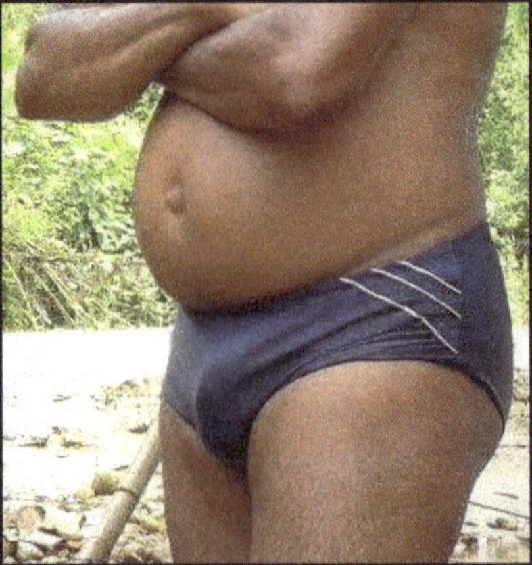

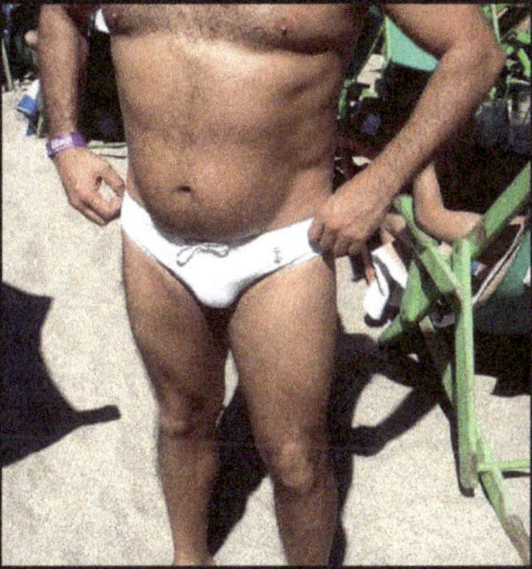

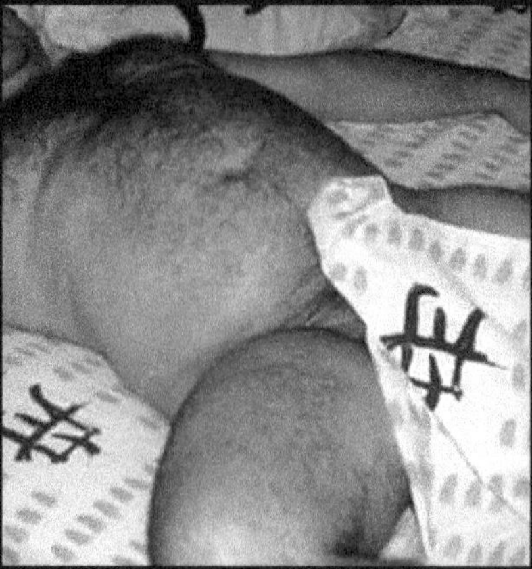

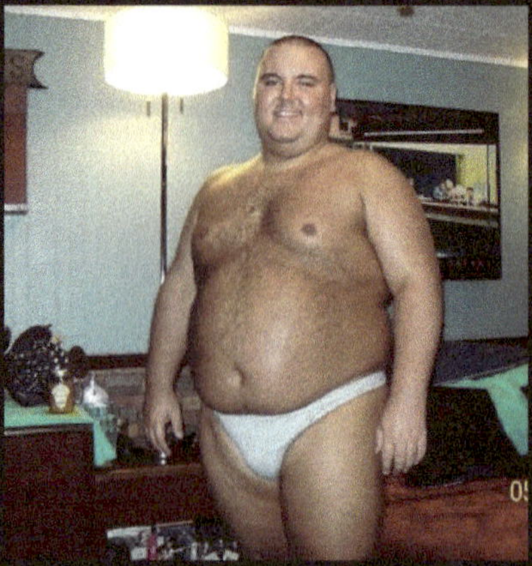

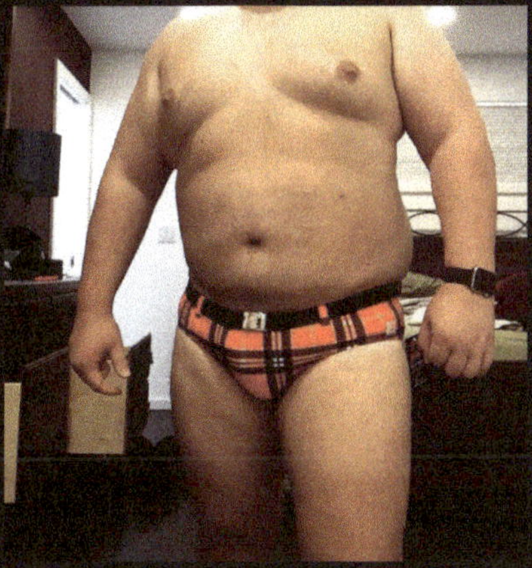

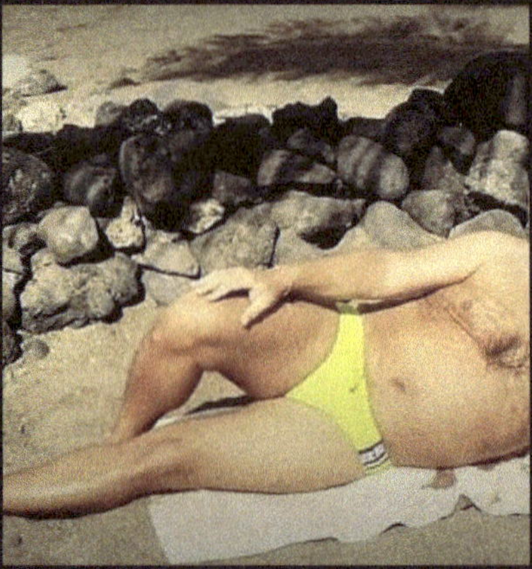

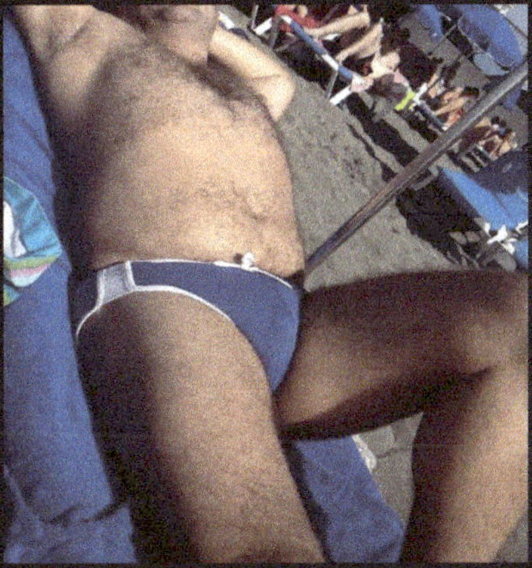

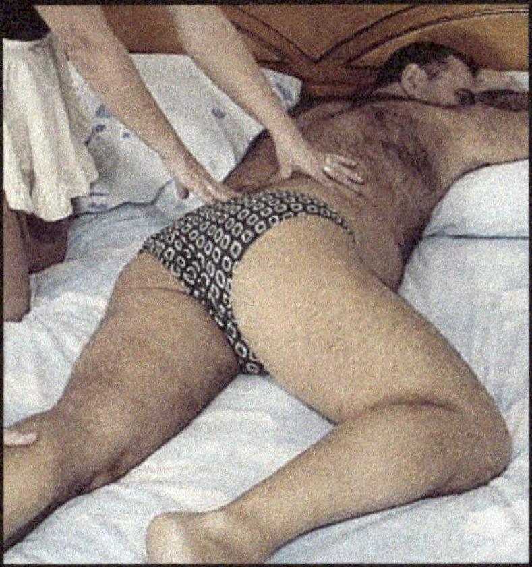

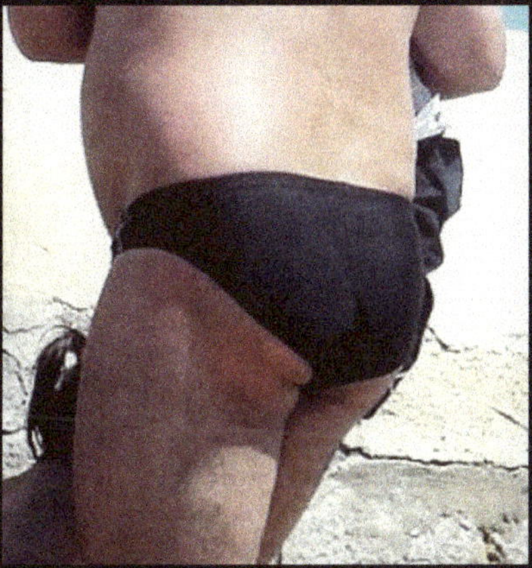

FEDERAÇÃO DOS
BRASIL
ASSOCIAÇÃO GERAL
E CULTURAL

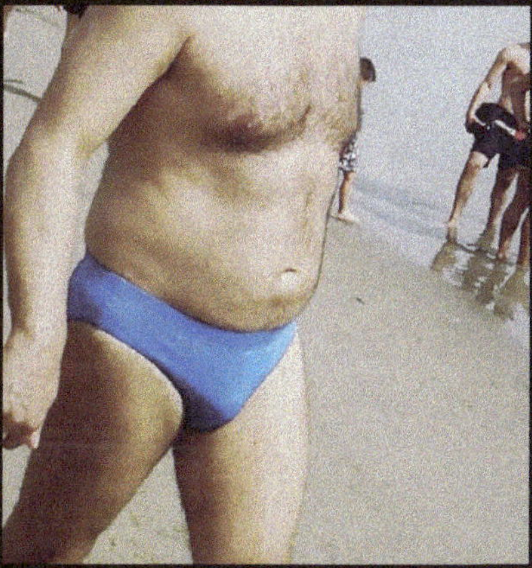

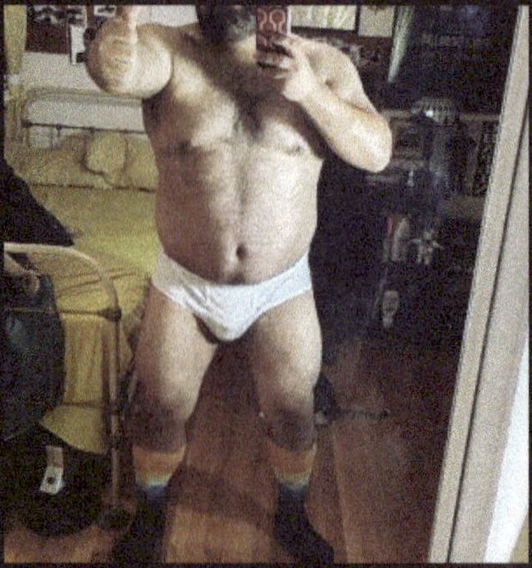

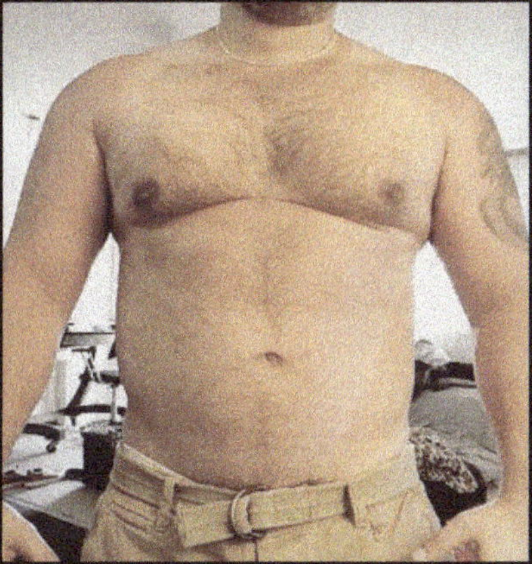

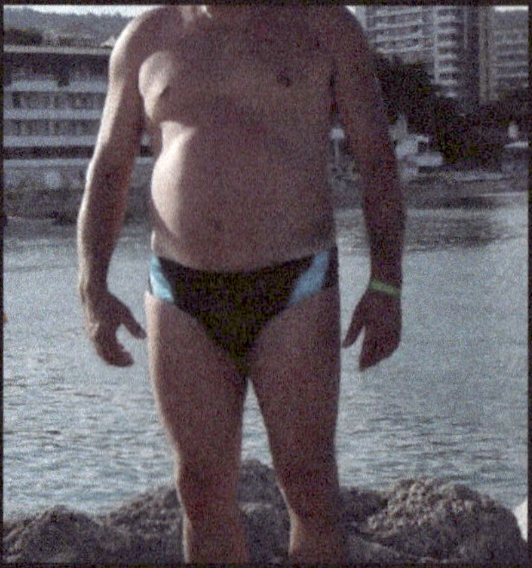

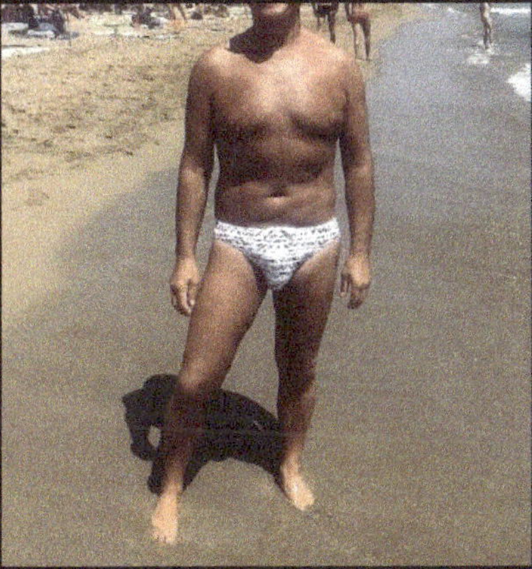

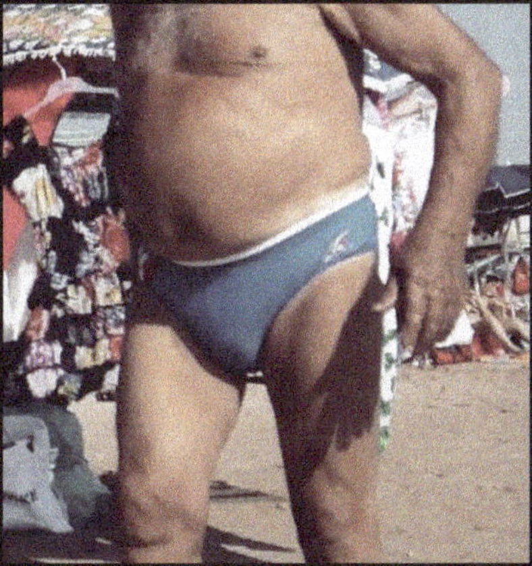

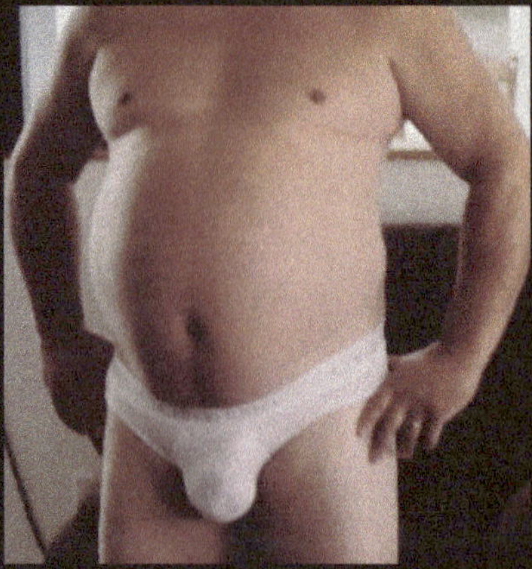

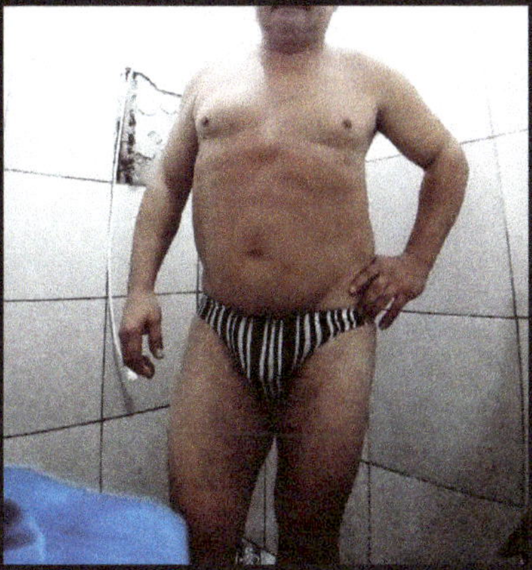

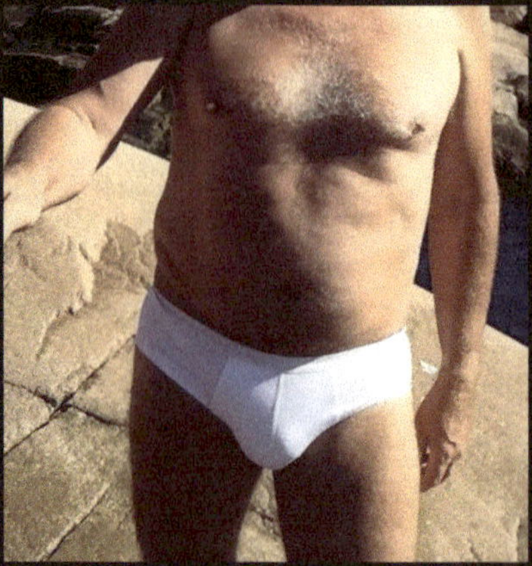

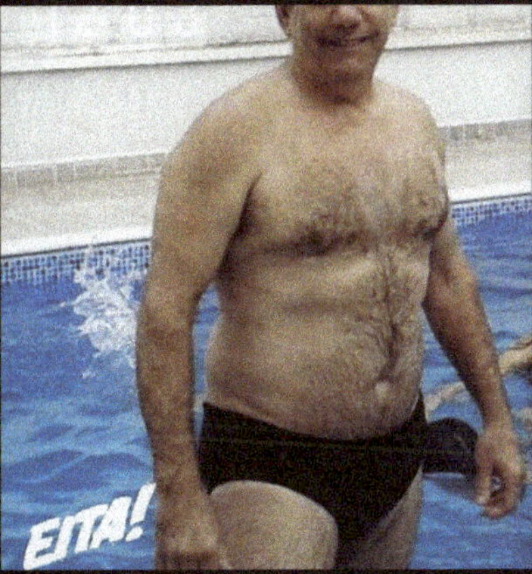
ΕΠΑ!

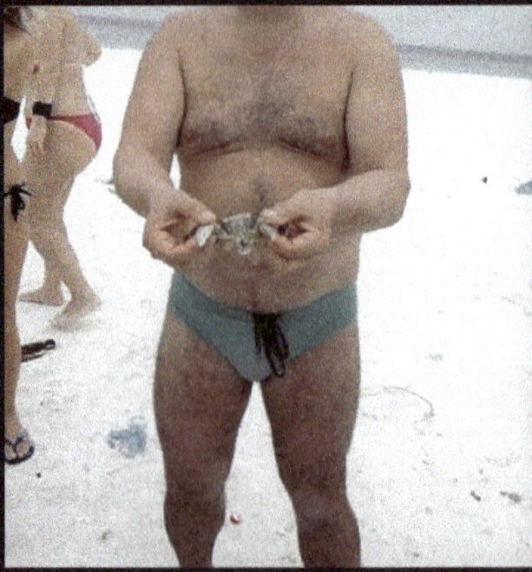

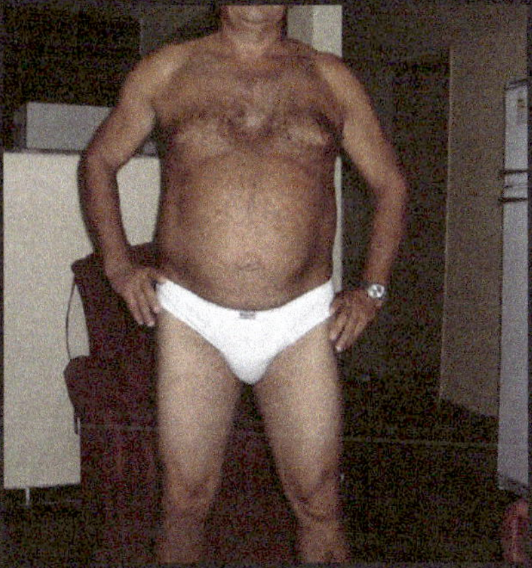

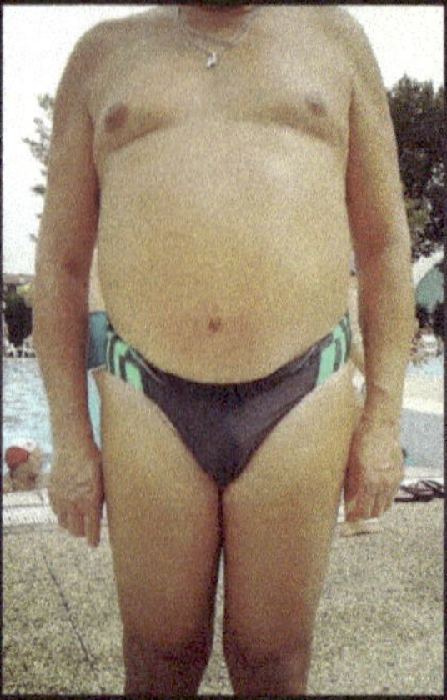

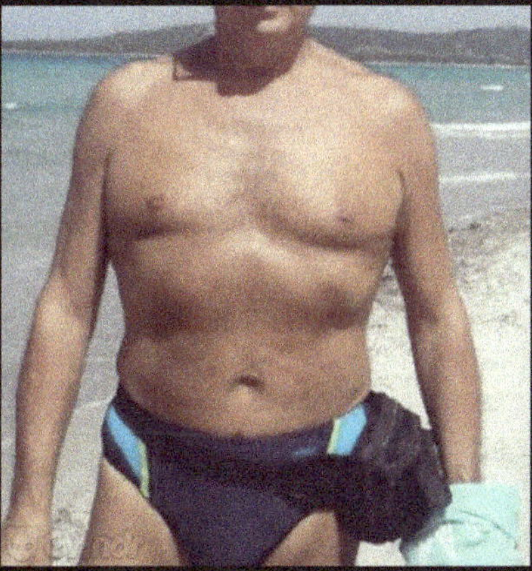

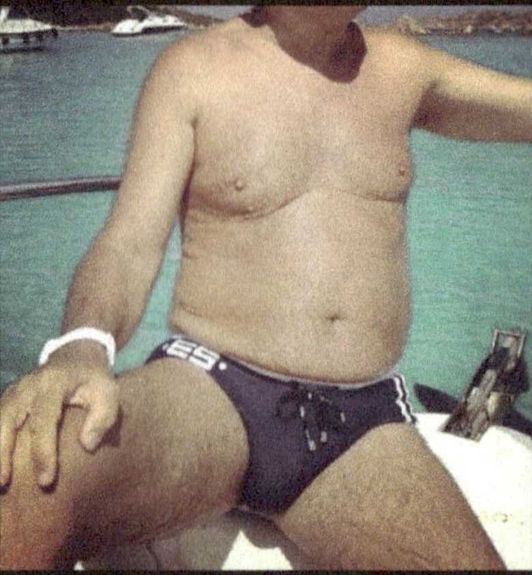

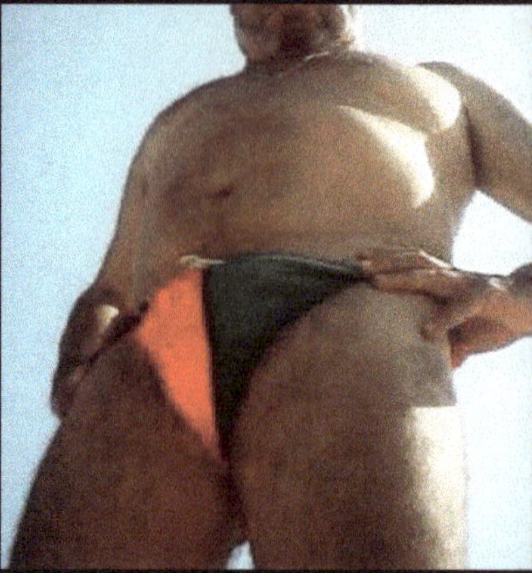

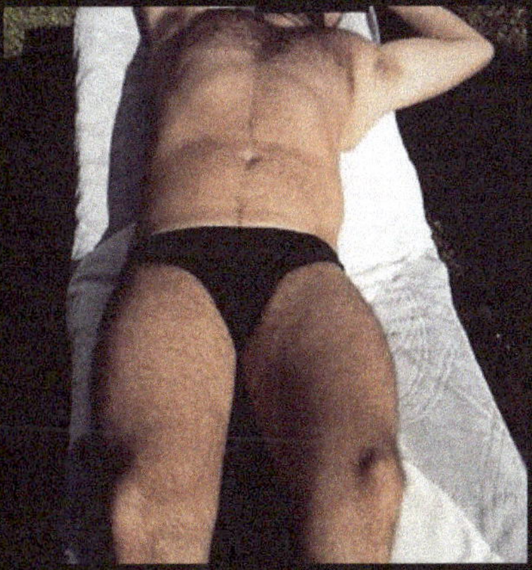

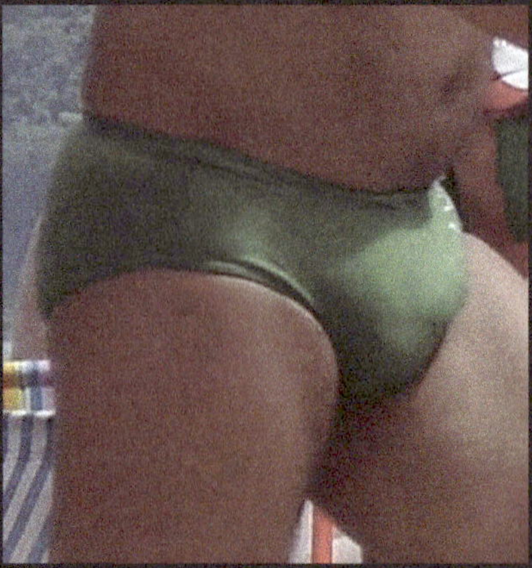

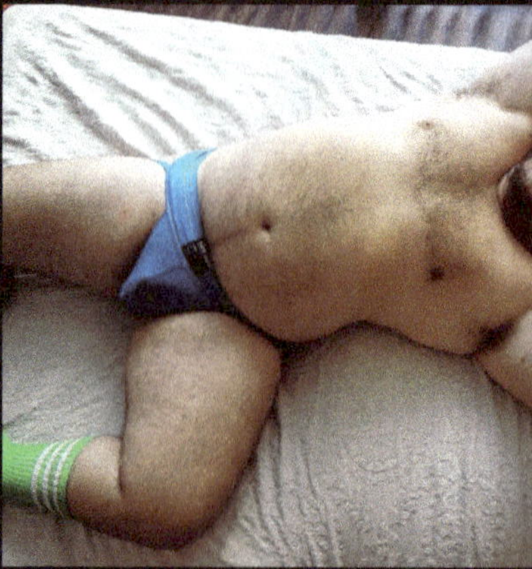

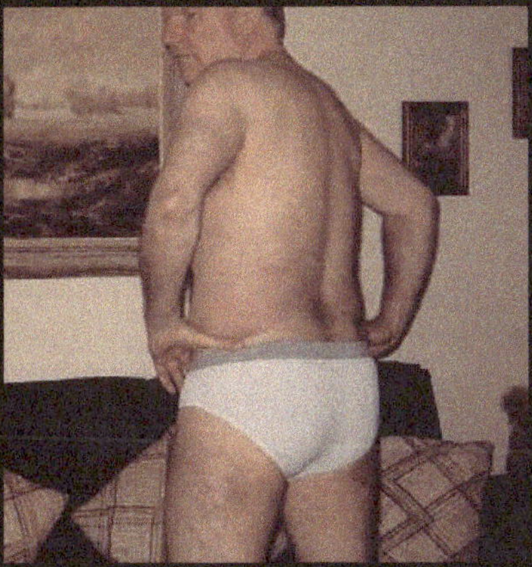

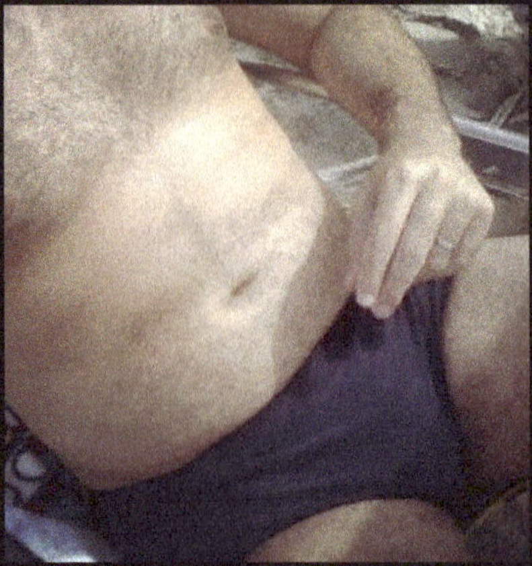

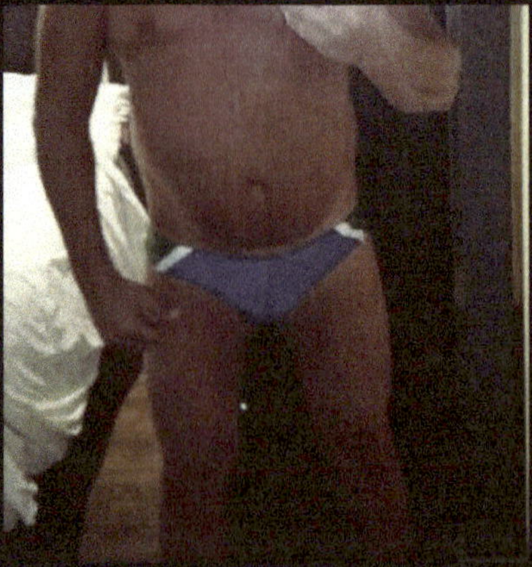

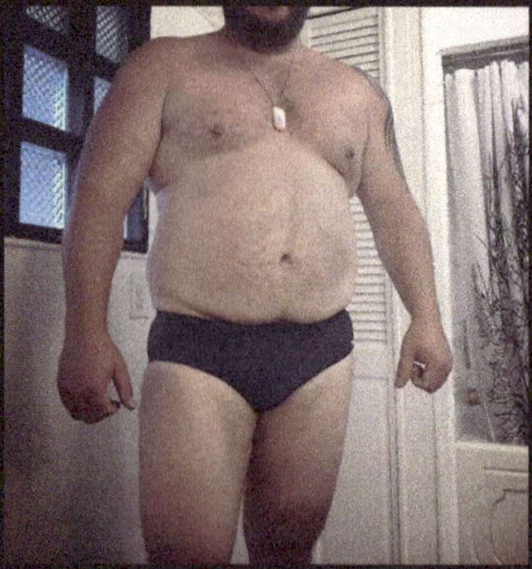

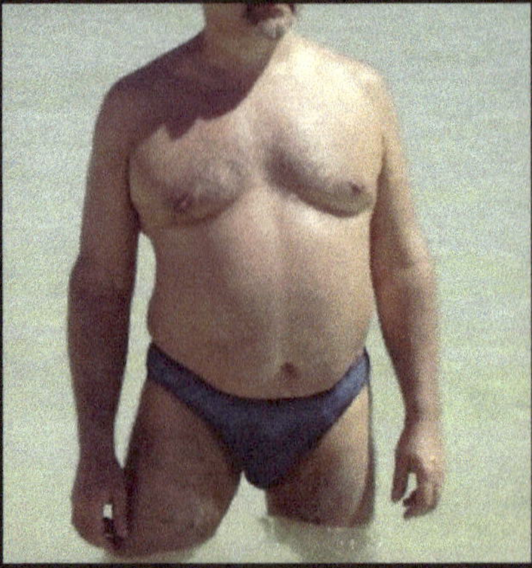

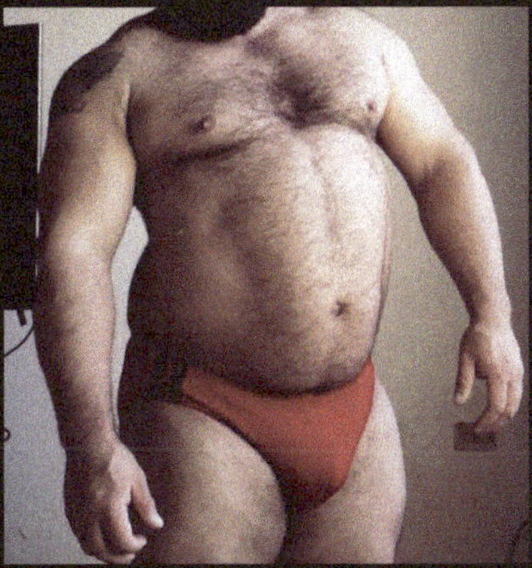

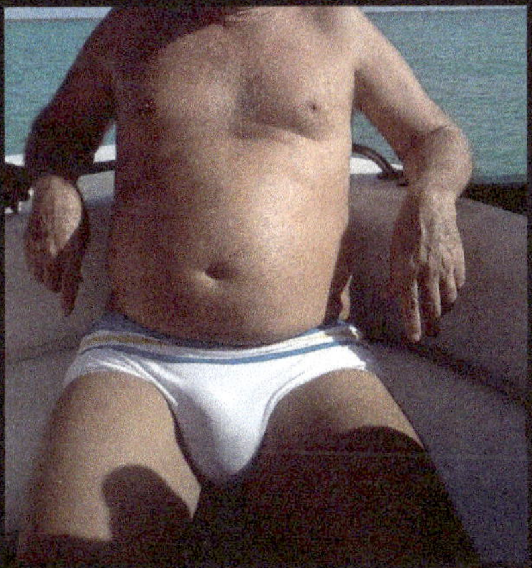

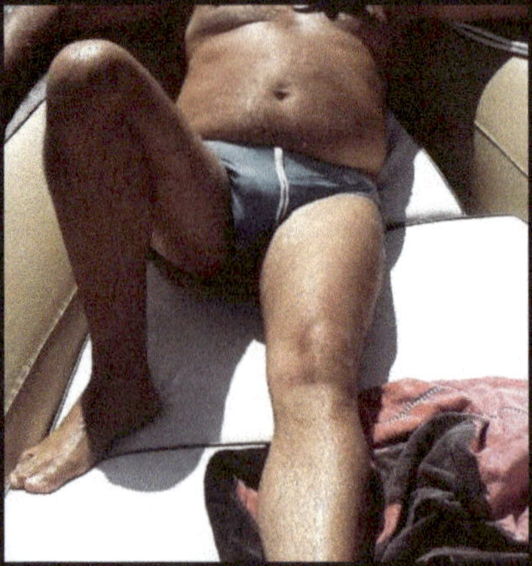

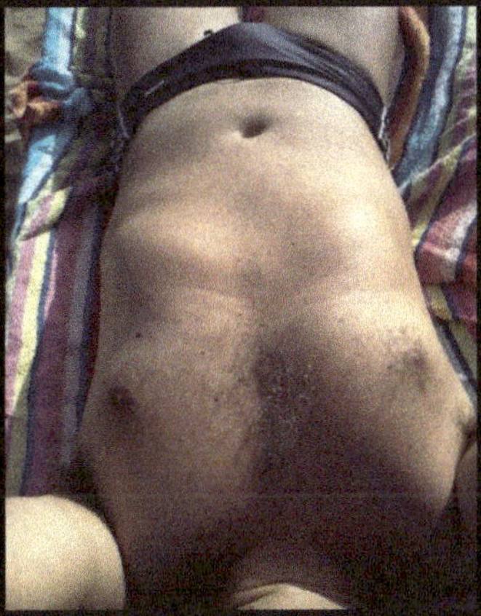

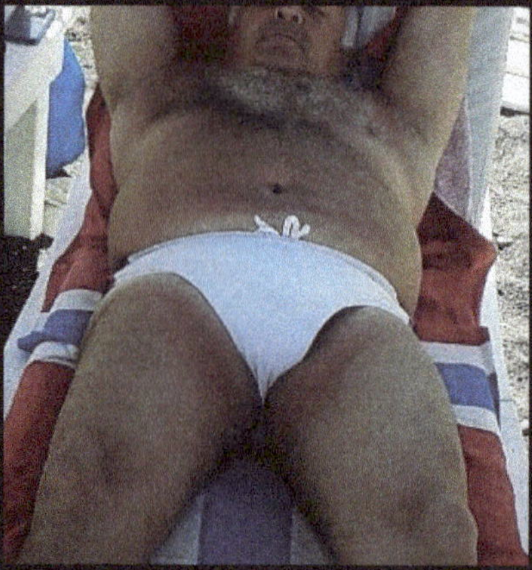

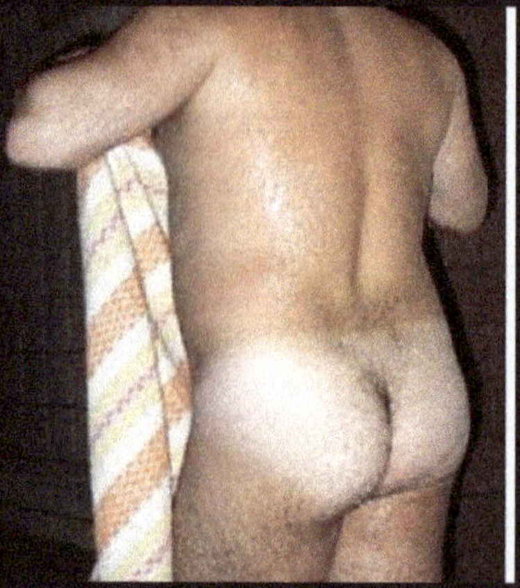

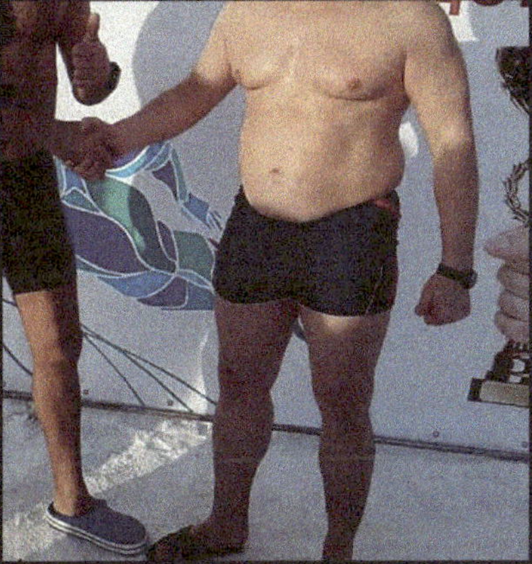

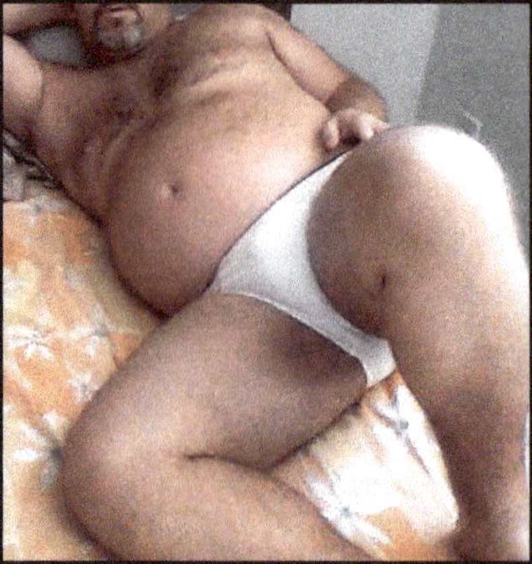

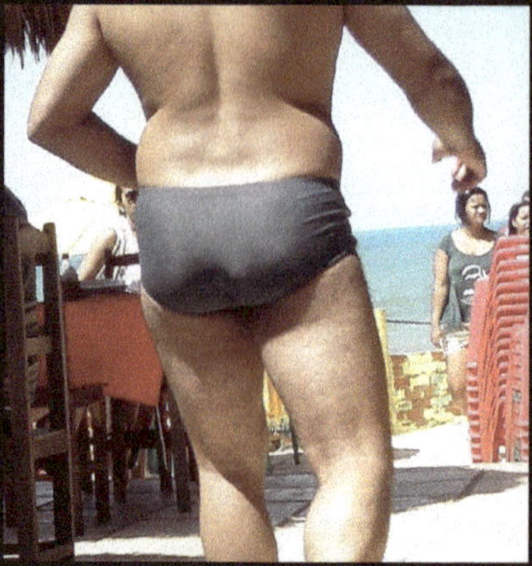

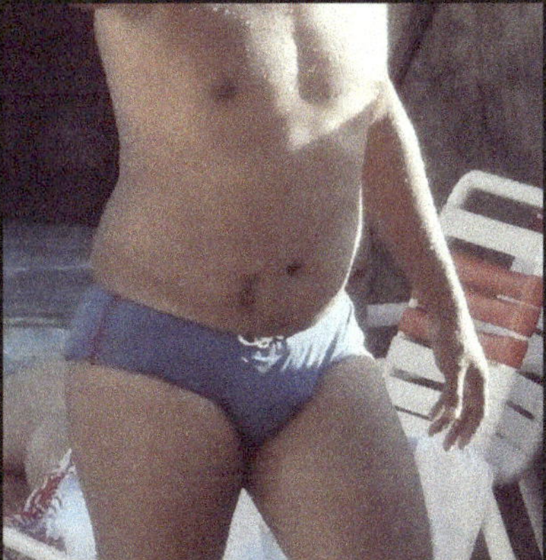

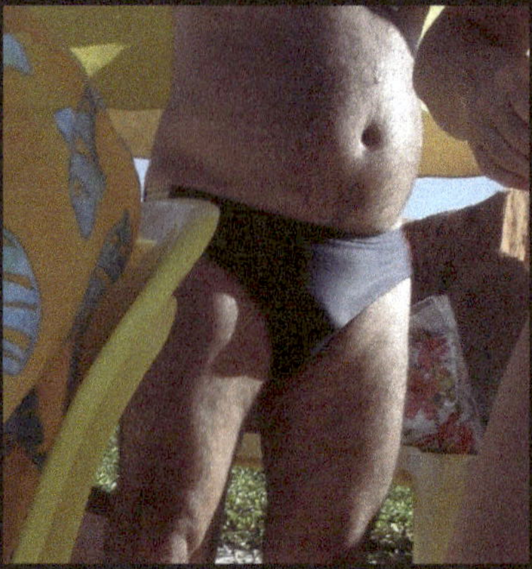

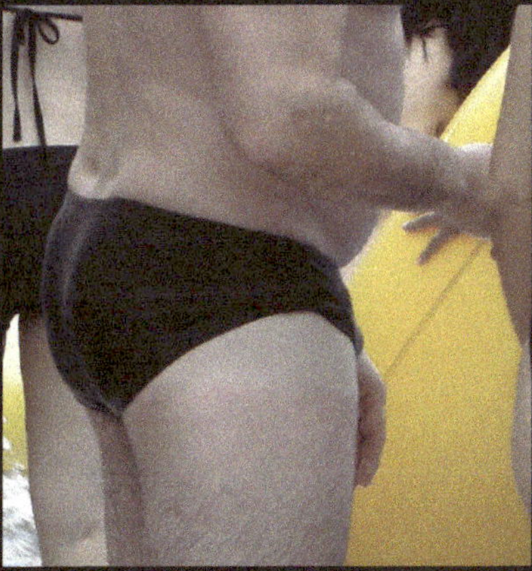

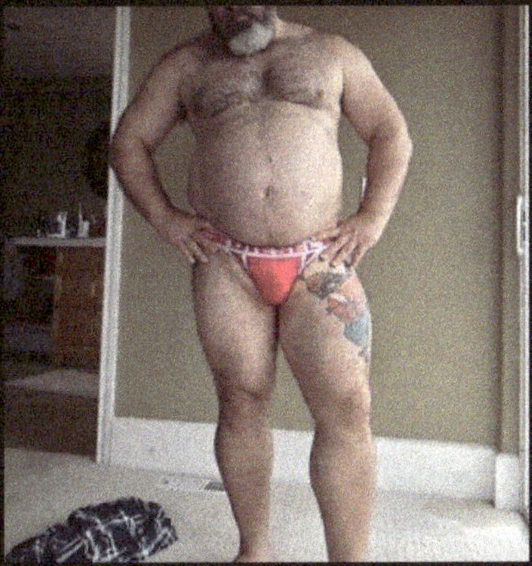

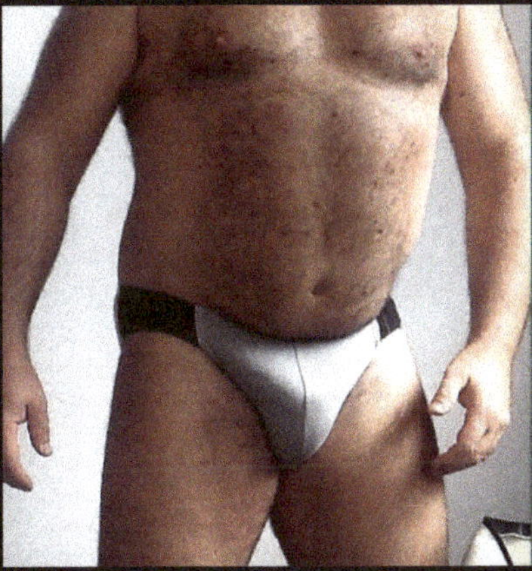

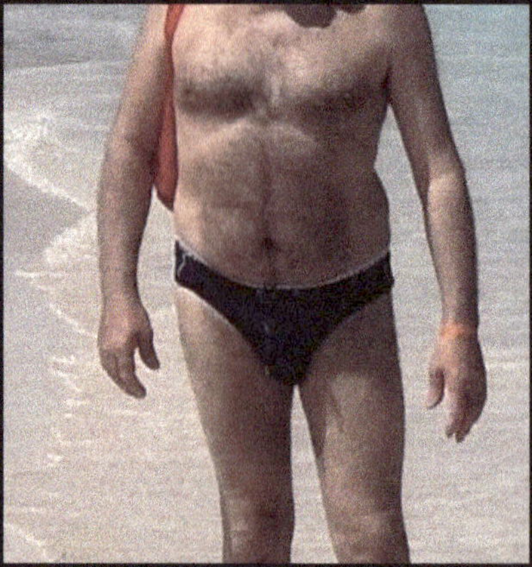

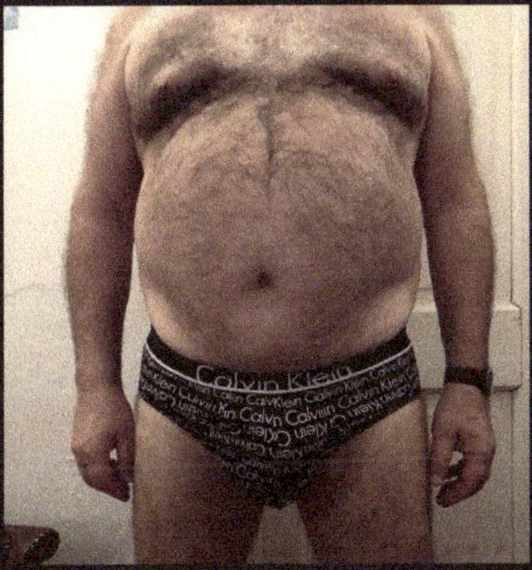
Calvin Klein

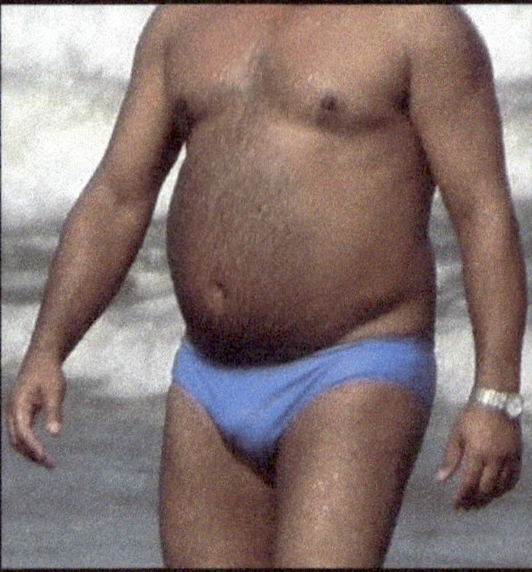

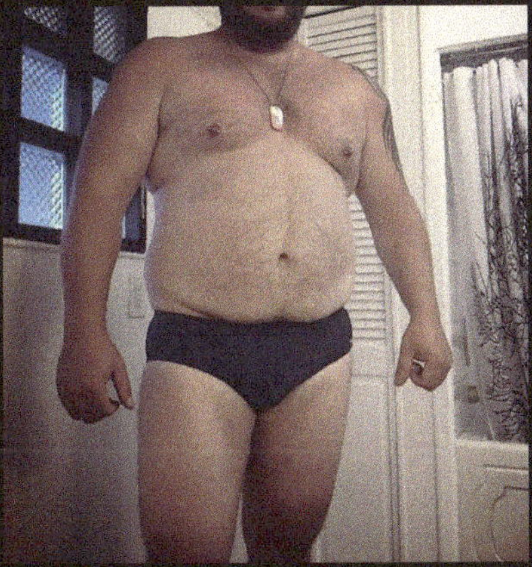

CPSIA information can be obtained
at www.ICGtesting.com
Printed in the USA
BVHW021904040419
544636BV00016B/119/P

9 780368 480829